V9
BOOK OF
LIVED

Penny Authors

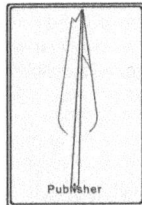

Publisher

MA PUBLISHER

Penny Authors

Copyright © Penny Authors 2023

Produced by MAPublisher for Penny Authors
Email: Pennyauthors@yahoo.co.uk
www.pennyauthors.org.uk

Published by MA Publishing (Penzance)
Email: mapublisher@yahoo.com
www.mapublisher.org.uk

Released on August 2023rev.2

Printed in the region the books have been published: Australia | Canada | Europe | UK | USA

ISBN-13: 9781915958037

Disclaimer:
All expressions and opinions of the work belong to the artists and PA does not share or endorse any other than to provide the open platform to publish their work. For further information on PA policies please email: pennyauthors@yahoo.co.uk for further information and submission guidelines.

Cover designed by Mayar Akash
Typeset in Times Roman

Paper printed on is FSC Certified, lead free, acid free, buffered paper made from wood-based pulp. Our paper meets the ISO 9706 standard for permanent paper. As such, paper will last several hundred years when stored.

2

CONTENT

Introduction 6
Roll Call 7
A Different World 10
Mental Hospital 11
Pain 12
Bits 13
Shaman Dalang 14
Vision 15
A Dream Of Night House 16
Unconditional Love From 1943 17
He Rebel 19
The Trapeze Artist 20
Jump 21
Solstice Haiku 22
The Drowning Man 23
Aroma Of Garlic 24
Tribute 25
No Time To Say Goodbye 26
Purpose 27
No More 28
Mellow 29
The Point 30
Like The Child You Are 31
Beauty 32
Found Myself 33
Profile 34
Sadly Love Is Never Enough 35
The Sun Scores Its Silver Blade 36
They Should Have Done It Yesterday 37
Night Poem 38
Hear Me 39
Wolf's My Feet 40
The Dust Storms Of The Soul 41
The Legend Of Port Quin 42
The Black Lake (From A Dream) 43
Broken Heart (A Prayer) 44
A Friendship Bursts 45
Tiger 46
Yum, Yum, Yum! 47
Train Travel 48

Mother's Funeral 49
Spring 50
Ode To A Blackbird 51
Agapanthus Africanus 52
Aglaisurticae Or Small Tortoiseshell Butterfly 53
Misumena Vatia (The Crab Spider) 54
The Boy Who Didn't Like Sand Between His Toes 55
I'll Always Be There 56
Eavesdropping 57
The Dad Dilemma 58
Honourable Mention 59
Magdalen 60
Sometimes 61
Solace 62
Grief 63
The Road Of Life 64
Palms 65
Breathe/Repeat 66
The Beaufort Scale 67
Dad 69
Simplicity 70
Flower Within 71
Verdant Temple 72
In God's House 73
Black Sheeps 74
Horse Whisper 75
Quiet 76
Queens Head! 77
The Moon 78
I Haven't Got A Clue 79
Reflections 80
Summer Solstice 81
The Day 82
Love Retreats 83
Painting By Numbers 84
Sagres Sunset 87
The Beauty Between Beauty And Beauty 88
Benjamin Mathew John Haddy 89
Ode To Alana 90
Schindler's Gist 91
Stormy Seas 92
Life 93

Time	94
Waking Up	95
Through The Window	96
Nature	97
Conversations From Imagination	98
The Disillusioned Young Mum	99
Affairs Of The Heart	100
The Winds Of Change	101
Your Smile	102
Heritage-Less	103
Phyllis Calls From Her Room	104
Probably	105
Mellow	106
Index	107

Introduction

Welcome to the 9th accomplishment of the Penny Authors' Anthology. The previous anthologies have laid and built a strong pathway for grass roots writers to take their maiden step to get their work championed in the national and global theatre of the written words.

The experiences that are captured in the anthology are colourful and the times that they've happened give it the flavour. PA wants to give to the world, the world within and show the abundances of our lives. We all ride, "the ride of life" from different points, perspectives, spectrum, but all travel to the heart, the centre of "what life is to Penny Authors".

The collections in these books you will feel and experience experiences that will take you in and out, emotionally, mentally and spiritually. All you have to do is allow yourself get on a ride that will become a merry-go-round then may turn to a roller coaster, it will take you through life of all ages and some be it familiar experiences and occurrences, to some out of this world or weird and something wonderful.

This is the ninth instalment of the "Book of Lived," that lets you live life along with yours. If you would like to get involved then email pennyauthors@yahoo.co.uk.

We at Penny Authors like to recognise, remind and remember all the Penny Authors that have taken part, past always and present and you can find the full list in the books and now we have our website where all poets published through PA have their own profile page, thus achieving our original goal. The following list is to introduce the newcomers who are featured in this volume are now listed on line. They bring with them refreshing and unique life they've lived for us to read, enjoy and experience; each to their own take. The newcomers are listed on the "Roll Call":

So see you on the other side email us on pennyauthors@yahoo.co.uk and visit our website: www.pennyauthors.org.uk

Finally, we hope you will enjoy reading the Book of Lived.

Roll Call

We at Penny Authors like to recognise, remind and remember all the Penny Authors that have taken part past always and present:

1. Mayar Akash (Founder)
2. Zainab Khan,
3. Paul Harvey,
4. Isaac Harvey,
5. Rebekah Vaughan,
6. Rabia Mehmood,
7. Tamanna Parveen,
8. Ellis Dixon-King,
9. Liam Newton,
10. Professor Muhammad Nurul Huque,
11. Kalam Choudhury,
12. Rashma Mehta,
13. Mathew Saunders Whiting
14. Akik Miah
15. Nirmal Kaur
16. Julie Archbold
17. Lora Ashman
18. John Robert Gordon
19. Julie Anne Wheeler
20. Late Joan Hodge
21. Ruth Lewarne
22. Bhupendra M. Gandhi
23. Nicki & Laura Ellis
24. Alga Statham
25. Jeremy J. Lovelady
26. Peter Fox
27. Jamal Hasan
28. Stephan Goldsmith
29. Clare Saunders Whiting
30. Sally Walker
31. Elsa Kiernanfox
32. Jaida Begum
33. Abdul Mannan
34. John Cynddylan Dillon
35. Suzette Reed
36. Sandra Sanjeet Green
37. Coral Dodsworth

38. Amitrajit Raajan
39. Chris York
40. Ossian Hughes
41. Stuart Cooper
42. Mustak Mustafa
43. Samiul Fox
44. Ayesha Chowdhury
45. Ferdous Rahman
46. Abu Maryam Gous
47. Steve Willoughby
48. Abul Hussain
49. Libby Pentreath
50. Paul Phillips
51. Adrian Smith
52. Paul Crump
53. Roger Lowry
54. Moriom Chaudhury
55. David Harley
56. John S. Wallis
57. Michael Ashton
58. Sabina Begum
59. Mary Fletcher
60. Rob Kersley
61. Tyrone M Warren
62. Alison Ali Norton
63. Andrew Harry
64. Janey Bryson
65. Paul Keeting
66. Res John Burman
67. Robyn Harry
68. Jade Carter-Bennet
69. Leo Rudman
70. Opu Islam
71. Eve Wakeling
72. Edwin Lewis
73. Tahi Chowdhury
74. Jenny Bishop
75. Angie Butler
76. Adrian Frost
77. Vivian Pedley
78. Robert Spencer
79. Pam Turner

80. Leema Begum
81. Chloe Hall
82. Keith Woodhouse
83. Alan S Whitfield
84. Sonja Fairfield
85. Daniel Munn
86. Penny Collins
87. Julie Flowerdew
88. Rosie Beale
89. Carol Bea
90. Ruth Husbands
91. Neil Graham Oats
92. Joanna Edwards
93. Antony Craig Oats
94. Bea Thompson
95. Nayma Chumchun
96. Jonathan Hayter
97. Mukut Borpujari
98. Francesca Owen
99. Lowenna Helen Kaute
100. Valerie Kaute
101. Christine Jilbert
102. Nicole Paton

For more information or if you would like to submit your work for inclusion, email: pennyauthers@yahoo.co.uk or visit our website: www.pennyauthors.org.uk

A Different World

Our climate isn't what it used to be,
Unseasonably weather and rising sea.
An abrupt climate shift is going ahead.
So there was some truth, in what the Mayans said.

As violent storms rage,
Sea levels rise,
Gigantic size hail falls from our skies.

As global temperatures get much higher,
Scorching heatwaves, catastrophic wildfires.

The impacts of climate change are now being felt
As polar ice cap continue to melt.
Nobody would listen to constant warnings,
From the devastating impacts from global warming.

From freezing blizzards, to catastrophic floods,
Unprecedented heatwaves to drought,
Stop global warming the protestors shout!

The sea temperatures are rising at an alarming rate,
Climate change is accelerating there's no time to wait.

Our animals and sea life are also at stake,
What shall be our planets fate.

Records being broken day in day out,
Constant warnings forecasters give out.

Cyclones, tropical storms we feel the wrath.
An unexpected hurricane changes its path.

Is that a tornado I hear you cry.
Debris and roofs suddenly fly by.
A tornado has unexpectedly touched down.
In a rural location, street or your town!!

Mental Hospital

Slamming doors, huge thumping sounds;
Prison officers standing all around
Medication that f**ks the psyche,
Tracksuit bottoms by Adidas or Nike
Day time television blaring out,
Psychosis is the removal of all self-doubt,
global telepathy in our heads,
Psychic sleeping in our beds
I sent a poem to a magazine
I take my Depakote and Thorazine
Permanent cigarette and cup of tea
Shaving mirror reflecting me.
What are those mansions of the mind?
What sort of people do we find?
Within these walls, sequestered away,
no one is going home today.
Threatened by high security,
Medicated mental purity,
The purity of raw violence,
how about some space and silence?

Pain

Every wound is festering
inching
seeping with anguish and despair
the stench
of exhausted rotten tormented flesh
gasping for air
gripping with fear.

Pumping ever pounding
temples pulsating rushing red cells
torment the carotid...
salty water drips...
confusion
turmoil
strummers silenced.

Memories fill the empty halls of justice
with rotten apples
in nooses heads hang upside-down
Seeds crushed distorted
crippled in extension
I didn't grow
as much as I pained.

Bits

It's the bits you miss that count
It's the spaces between the objects you draw
Tears that howl for comfort in the tempest
Call
Hunger for your notice silently clothe your naked thoughts
underneath and above in the swirl of all. It's not what you say
that counts, unless like some sad lonely leaning rusted capstan,
once used to fasten the sailing ships to shore,
You mark by your very failing existence the way the estuarial
Moon-loved tide turns on the changing shore

Commentary: "Who's she then? I like her song, I liked the violin and the squeezebox too. And the pirate who played them and the money in his pulled-off shoe."

"She's a lapsed dancer," says Heyoka, "that's all we got.
She says she's from Misfits just south of Plymouth Rock."

Aphrodite blows that purple smoldering smoke ring; it hovers like a halo thought...

...bits, bits of what we've been taught

Shaman Dalang

In the other room darkness prevails,
Covers the animals from their heads to their tails!
I hear the Dalang calling,
He my master,
I am on all fours crawling,
I shape- shift into a Jaguar,
In the room the Dalang is performing,
He my master, I hear him calling!
As I make it behind the curtain,
He calls me to him,
I am on all fours crawling,
I am not a man,
But a shaman bawling,
This the moments calling,
Lift the shadows in the light,
Just at fall of night!

Vision

The night was over
And the sea curds crackled
And bent,
crisply, in the deadening rays
Of morning,
As she sank into the bank
Of the sand speckled
Tulip blossom
And angry
Red spangled pupil sun.
The flat marram pools
spoke lizards
To the turkey sitting on an egg yolk.
Country chunk animals
Jumping,
Sheep hopping over styles
And farm-captained land
Grand and handsome
In the green wheat field
Sun shaken fairy-tale,
Magic castle,
Dancing,
Peopled and happening.

A Dream Of Night House

It's winter
And grow dark,
We go to the night bed
And starts
Weird rattles and giggles

And the home
Wakes up it rustles, rattles, shudders, shakes
The night house
As a haunting monster

So starts
Stretches arms, legs
Does a wild tap dance
With a sly
Little smile on face

And sometimes
Hear chatter, chatter
Give a fright
Try to go
Back to sleep

Alarm starts
Seven o'clock
Night house goes mad
Antics
Suddenly stop.

Wonder
Did night house move
at all?
Was it just a dream?

Unconditional Love from 1943

Last week my Nan decided it was time
to sign off for good on the dotted line,
and while her carer's call was sad, indeed
condolences are just so hard to read:
'She's finally at peace.' 'It's for the best.'
'She's no longer in pain.' 'She's now at rest.'
And worst by far is, 'You can now move on.'
Such words are meant to comfort, now she's gone,
but I don't want to move on anywhere!
She was my Nan, I want to feel despair.

Her living room is as it's always been,
the faded olive carpet vacuumed clean,
her stick's still hooked over the fire grate,
her favourite chair with plumped cushions awaits
the carriage clock's chime from the mantle piece
but its hand movements also slowed and ceased.
Frozen in this hushed, suspended silence
time is paused in circumspect defiance.
You'd think that Nan's popped out to make some tea,
that any moment she'll be back with me.

I used to sit with her when I was young,
she'd ask about my days at school among
my friends, and how my half-term tests had been
and how my teachers were, and school routine.
Then we would look through photographs and smile
at my Great Uncle John, dressed in such style,
and her giggling sisters. Then my young Nan
herself, so full of life and of life's plans
waved through the lens from 1943.
Though twelve years old, she was waving to me.

Each month I would visit my Nan at home,
or send warmest greetings over the phone.
Now family occasions through the year
will never feel the same as she's not here.
Hardest will be her birthday in July,
when midsummer's dry warmth lights up the skies.

Soon sadly her things will be packed away,
and I'll no longer need to go to stay,
and strangers will live in her house instead,
you see, it's for the living not the dead.

So, I've resolved on something I must do
to cherish Nan, and our memories too.
From time to time when I'm feeling downcast
I'll sit alone and delve into the past.
Great Uncle John will still smile back at me,
and Nan's sisters will always laugh with glee.
Something I know I can rely upon –
and draw love unconditionally from –
is Nan's warmth radiating back to me
in that photo from 1943.

He Rebel

With a flagrant disregard for existing social norms,
something's brewing in the anvil of thought.
Wild rhododendrons and bougainvilleas running
along the wall,
as we denounce the barriers of casteism and marginalization.
No to the elite.
No to centuries of limiting beliefs and traditions,
their insistence—the shackles of our own minds.
At midnight,
in the waning light of the stars in the sky,
the silhouette of our necks interlocked like flamingos.
I miss you. I never even met you:
let us take a deep dive into our imaginations,
until we find the right imagery and metaphors
we can discuss—dissect;
not for ego's sake, but for love.

The Trapeze Artist

She needs no introduction
From a top hatted, scarlet coated Ringmaster
As she clings to her silken trapeze.
She has no call for jugglers or acrobats
That might enhance her performance
Nor clowns that dance and throw
Fake water into the audience
None of those can ever alter her regal pose
She's lashed her line between the olive tree
And the weathervane
High up in the stratosphere of my backyard
In order to gain an advantage over her unwary prey.
Each time she rewires the link she walks the tightrope
And hones her skill on the high wire.
She's a tireless performer, an arachnid charmer
She's not the smartest act in the show
But whenever the wind blows through
She fixes her harness, adjusts her armour
And becomes a Trapeze Artist.

Jump

Jump out of the box,
Into your Sox,
Jump out of the door,
Let's do it some more.

Jump if you get the hump,
And shake shake,
It will get you awake.

Jump in your head,
Out of your ear,
Onto the floor,
But careful you don't make yourself sore.

Jump pump up the best,
Get on the heat,
And make it a tweet.

Jump back into the box,
Conform to the rules,
And use their tools,
Pretend to be sane,
Until it's time,
To jump again.

Solstice Haiku

Golden zenith sun,
Celestial rays caress,
Lush verdant hedgerows,

Blossoming flowers,
Invite mass pollination,
Honeybees oblige.

Birds hatch sky-blue eggs,
Cocooned butterflies emerge,
Wings fluttering free.

Rosy-streaked skyline,
Dusk fireside celebrations,
Farewell,
Solstice sun.

The Drowning Man

Wild eyes,
Sea glass,
The drowning man,
Tugs me under,

Holdfast,
First of stone,
Viridescent weed,
Torn asunder.

Jettisoned love,
Subterranean blue,
Sea worn,
Halcyon slumber.

Aroma of Garlic

This makes me quite nostalgic,
Happy and sad merged together.
Side by side,
In an outdoor market,
Cotignac square in The Var, France,
And clear fountain,
Dried smoked,
And fresh garlic,
Wishing now you were still with me,
But it is not so.

Tribute

Tribute to Auntie Valerie
A premature farewell was said by you
Our time got cut short + All too soon you were
They brought you back home and I guess that you knew
The angels would meet you before very long
and so it was, as you bid us goodbye,
To let go of your earthly pain,
Now your spirit is free + your soul to fly high,
until such time as we meet again...
Dedicated to my auntie Valerie,
released from her pain in the early hours of Friday 16th January 2004,
after a brave and noble battle fought with cancer...
"you were a real fighter – tough as old boots and strong as an Ox!!
Such strength and perseverance as you demonstrated in your lifetime
has been great inspiration to us all".
"your friendly nature and cheerful disposition touched many hearts and won you
many friends.
People have described how bubbly, happy and full of life you were.
Your straight forward, honest approach to dealing with
your ongoing fight with cancer can only be testimony as to just how admirable
you were.
"You'll shine on with the stars in heaven now, just like you shone here on earth"

No Time to Say Goodbye

I had to leave quite suddenly
no time to say goodbye
The journey, once it had begun
went on and on.
And it became quite beautiful
Once on the other side.
But once I reached my destiny,
though beautiful, I knew,
That I could not return to you,
twas then my sadness grew,
yet I was only sad because
you could never know
that I would be beside you now
for always until you
Begin the journey I have made
And when you reach this side,
I'll be waiting patiently
with love so deep and true,
That if you knew what I know now
My joy would be yours too.

Purpose

I walk on the path to nowhere,
to find my purpose,
and to reach somewhere,
keep walking on,
and on,
It may take years before the calm,
your mind doesn't give up,
fills your head,
no let up.
"Stop!"
I shout!
Stop!
Let it all out,
Let it go,
That cold north wind blows.

A nip to your ear,
A whisper of a song,
Very music from your soul listen,
Can you hear?
Sit alone staring out at nature
as far as the eye can see
Beauty and peace let it be,
Let it be.
A silence falls
just the breeze and the beauty of it all,
t's a perfect, a picture of the living world,
most Will never truly see,
and live, to feel truly free.

No More

Everyone
judges
So when they
judge
show
them
something
great
so they
judge
no more

Mellow

Soft
Sweet
and full flavoured
Gentle
Relaxation to music
gentle touch
ripe fruits looks nice to eat
reference to wine
mild curry
hot summer
savoury rice
soothing throat
aged older
perfect people
ripened fruits
arrive on time
grow plants
water falls
calm and cheerful
makes you happy
soften nature
calming and relaxing
and birds singing

The Point

Today, I woke in pain,
as usual
I dragged myself out of bed,
and dressed.

What's the point?
I thought.

The point!
is my friends,
my daughter,
my sister,
then the sun shone.

And all is good in my world.

Like The Child You Are

The sea doesn't care if you're having a bad day,
but it can help,
without it even knowing your state of mind.
It goes in and out of its way, to wash away your tears,
soothe the sadness, or seethe and agree with your wrath and anger.

It is always there for you, breathing deeply
and listening without judgement.
It mirrors your quiet days, laps up your grief like a trusty hound.
It curls itself easily around jagged rocks,
smooths over the pebbles of despair
weighing you down in your helplessness
and lets anger float away into the sunset.

It can tickle your feet and make you laugh,
like the child you are,
and carry you feather light and help you fly,
reflect every mood and make a bad day bearable,
when nothing else works.

When nothing else works,
the sea can match the saltiness of your tears
and save your sad life, and make you a carefree child again.

Beauty

I think the clouds are so beautiful
the way they formed in the brightly,
daylight sky.

When the rain lashes down so hard
the clouds turn to thick and grey.

When the sun comes out the clouds go bright
and you can see them better in the daylight then at night.

But the sky turns bright when you see the Sheppard's delight in the
middle of the night.

Oh what a sight to see the beautiful daylight and night in its shining
glory and might.

Found myself

You are making me cry
You are making me nervous
You are keeping me wonder around
You are the cloud in the sky.

You are giving me a purpose in my life
You are making me proud
You are making me smile you are the music in the air
You are the Sunshine in my life,
Since the day you walked into my life
I am not the same person
I have lost myself into your heart
But no regrets
I found the peace,
love and happiness
I found everything that I
only could dream of.

Profile

We are sexual, telepathic, word orientated goofs,
We are nebulous, necromantic, prehensile,
We are roaming, reared and romantic,
We are benign, bovine and bizarre,
Our residencies are eclectic,
Places, like time, happen anywhere.
We have free will yet constantly fight our own destiny,
And cannot subjugate matter over fidelity,
We are born to remember ourselves,
Holding statue in the face of volition,
The road is fraught with danger,
We are supernuminaries on the stage of the world theatre,
Human life is both precious and dispensable,
The societies that have occurred are meretricious,
Tribal chaos veneered by bouncing colour,
Adult schizomania rages, civilisation's final stages,
We are lumpen incarnate, mind-altered,
The world is a representation of our complexities,
By computer programmed serendipity,
And we are myriad, scattered, running,
Peopled by a thousand continents,
Jolly on the hop, a multi-faceted being.

Sadly Love Is Never Enough

Sadly love is never enough,
in the depth of a lifetime
in the still waters of time.

Love's soothing oil can often
calm the storms, the rising tide,
the crashing waves, but

when mistrust and hurt pinch,
too many times,
when jealousy and doubt,
lie like doormats in your way,

when the stars clash,
and time's candle flickers
in the draughts of anger,

love is never enough.

The Sun Scores Its Silver Blade

The sun scores its silver blade
on the still waters of the distant horizon.
The waters rise to the dark clouds of nowhere,
Silver blades from the sunbursts of everywhere.

Rains fall amongst the glittering crystal
on the moody sea of our view.
The hint of a promised rainbow appears
on the darkened luminous ocean,
and eternal greatness frames
this power of endless still time.

Troubles leave their wet footprints
to dry in the warmth of friendship,
laughter and delight balance
on the wheels of tomorrow, future hopes
lead to promise of better times,
as trust,
takes on its own shape with confidence.
And the sun scores its silver blade
on the still waters of the distant horizon.

They Should Have Done It Yesterday

We've watched them, over and over,
the wrong turns they've taken,
the wrong choices they've made, or

in fact they appear to see no choice at all,
when they should have been watching,
planning, preparing for the future.

We step lightly in our parents footsteps.
We learn from the mistakes of others.
We see with the eyes of the ancestors,

hope, success, fulfilment, comfort,
they come in many disguises.
These fools ignore the signs at their peril,

and suffer for it,
because, they should have made choices,
taken the right turns,

they should have done it yesterday.

Night Poem

Have you ever heard the sound
of the deep dark night.
How it dances with your shadow
in the cold starry night.
Synchronicity like two feathers
entwined in the breeze
the secret silence hidden in
beneath the sound of trees.

No one around in the dark
ambience of its belonging
not even a sound.

That sweet secret
stillness of nothing
that ringing through
your ears deafening.

...Or

The fear of blindness
in its deep pitch.

Can anybody hear me,
is anyone around
...not a pin drop
not even a sound.

Hear Me

Hear the name of my voice
the way it vibrates
through the letters and
curls around the tongue
echoing through the hollow gullet
and bellow through the waves and
falls upon death ears
I wish you could feel my words
penetrate through your psyche
and slide neatly in to your consciousness
reaching deeply into your beautiful soul.

Wolf's my Feet

Empty shells with deep pockets
wollets filled magical plastic
tap tap, beeb beeb
those pockets cavernous
leave the river Baron
not even a drop to give the wolf's and snake's at my feet.
They need to feed thirsty for the pound
Not satisfied with a shilling.

The Dust Storms of the Soul

I walk into the madness with an acceptance that chaos rules this moment,
It's the end of a cycle,
Outside a storm is raging,
Inside my heart is aching,
No more mirrors to reflect, refract and refer to,
All is in shadow, cast in night,
Here I go, ragged and broken,
A shaken bottle never to be opened,
My mouth trying to frame the words,
Competing with my heart for sustenance and growth,
All is up for destruction and resurrection in new forms,
But I cannot hold the gaze,
My eyes sore from the dust storms in the soul,
No one knows where to go!

The Legend of Port Quin

I see your pale face at the small cottage window
Your sad eyes always looking far over the sea
Searching the skyline for the fishing boats coming
But there'll be no more homecomings for you and for me.

Every man in the village was out for the fishing
Every boat in the village was out on the sea
When the weather came storming in from the nor' west
Now there'll be no more homecomings for you and for me.

Grandfathers, Fathers and their sons now just learning
The hard ways of fishing and working the sea
In one short afternoon, so suddenly taken
So there'll be no more homecomings for you and for me.

Every man in the village so suddenly drown-ded
Every wife, every girl now a widow must be
And now each small cottage window is suddenly tear stained
There'll be no more homecomings for you and for me.

I was young and was strong and was happily married
My young wife would sing her sweet love songs to me
Now I see her in black in the small tear stained window
There'll be no more homecomings for I'm lost at sea.

I see your pale face at the small cottage window
Your sad eyes still looking far over the sea
For three hundred years still searching the horizon
But there'll be no more homecomings for you and for me.

I've watched as the slates from the roofs began slipping
Watched as the weeds grew where we played happily
But still I see your dear face in the small cottage window
As I watch from my berth here in the stormy grey sea.

(Fading)
There'll be no more homecomings for you and for me.
No scones by the fire as you pour me my tea
No singing me love songs as you sit on my knee
There's no more homecomings for you and for me.

The Black Lake (from a dream)

I can fly,
Right at the forefront,
Is it the temporal lobe?
Think it is, it manifested it,
Drawn skyward driven by the will, determination,
The more I will it, the faster I go,
I've seen it and been it in dreams,
I hover and fly above the frozen black lake,
Enormous, frozen, it's an oxbow shape,
'Look I can fly! '
I fly into the hideaway of Kohl -eyeliner- leering youngsters, like zombies they
are drugged by their sleep,
'I made the lake black, dropping ink into its depths, flying over it' I cry,
But they are not impressed,
Instead they turn their venomous eyes on to different prey,
I fly over it again, the lake,
Could be a Welsh valley, or lake Bala, or somewhere like that,
Made black by peat,
A sudden loss of power and I break it's icy surface.
Then I wake up.
The Lake is deep and dark,
The Lake is deep and dark,
The Lake is deep,

Broken Heart (A prayer)

Once again I am doing penance for my sins,
Taking apart the heart and digging the knife in,
Showered in blood the wounds so recently healed,
Covered all in a red curtain-like cloak I swear saw Christ in,
I broke my heart by playing this fools game,
Behind the mask of lying and cheating I shredded the velvet screen,
I gazed on that which was not meant to be;
Venus in Virgo; agape and me
The love that was unconditional,
(Is in my star scene, (seen))
Was not,
But there she was upon her pedestal in the Lady Chapel,
behind the rood screen,
The truth was...
Lambs tails,
In spring,
Every night I beat myself
Counting sheep,
And letting the sleep in,
'Dear Lord in heaven,
To never forget a betrayal; or a broken heart,
Forever and ever,
Amen,'

A Friendship Bursts

He walked straight towards me,
Every step made a crack on the dusty ground.
Not even once did I dare look at his heated face.
His words hurried out wildly from his mouth.
Like a Conflagration.
His screwed up eyes blazing into the atmosphere.
Blending with the storm performing clouds,
His anger cracking my crystal heart.
Was he too blind to see my sorrow?
My head was twisting round and round
Tumble-drying the brainstorm
Filled with darkness of lost passion.
Tears held tightly behind the discrimination,
My lips faltered,
The words to let out
Trapped in my throat.
The explosion of fear
Is a thirst too strong to be slaked?
I am trapped and lost in a nowhere land
Where it is too late for mercy.

Tiger

There was a tiger,
As stripped as a jumper, orange and black
He was proud of himself,
A figure with a powerful and
Moving back

Tiger I have always wished I had a coat like yours
Shall I come near you
and touch it?

But, of course you will not bite
Are you sure?
You catch my eyes

Yum, Yum, Yum!

He was a rat and she was a rat.
His nose was as long as a ruler
Her nose was as small as a pin
He underground and she in some bushes.

He had a tail and she had a tail
His tail was as sharp as a knife.
Her tail was thick as a basketball bat
'What's that smell?'

He smell some cheese
She smell some cheese
His cheese was as bright as stars.
Her cheese was as dark as night

He crept out from underground.
She crept out from some bushes.
They searched for a meal 'Yum, Yum, Yum'
A cat came along 'Yum, Yum, Yum!'

Train Travel

How you would love this
TV about trains to Cornwall

My eyes start smarting
Remembering your wild enthusiasm
For trains
For me
The fun we had
You bounding off securing seats
Fetching tea for two
A searing pain
Wax ripped
Off the insides of my soul

The lost sweetness
Of shared love
The strong fortress
We built over the years

I'm torn apart
Pain in my heart
How could you die?
Not coming home ever.

Nafplion will still be there, you said
Cancelling that last holiday
And so it will.
'I can't find anyone'
I can't find anyone like you
to love me so
to love me through and through
I can't live long enough
for grief to fade
and tears to stop
until my turn to die
I don't mind when
Tonight would do
although I don't believe I'll meet you then
There'll be no such love for me again.

Mother's Funeral

Yellow roses - a large bunch tied
with black ribbon from my Valentine flowers,
the day you died - my fragile mother -
always strong
and a blue label on which I wrote those words you loved
that life flies, that the flower blooms and dies
I leave out for those that know the lines
'one thing is certain and the rest is lies.'

Here we are surrounded by those promises
those certainties that still don't make them smile - never -
and why don't they if they believe she'll live forever?
Everyone else's stiff arrangements from the florist
but mine have heads not impaled on wires
a bouquet of long-stemmed roses with sharp thorns.

Spring

I can't believe what the sun wrote
For the valley's lackluster vistas
Something

About the musky scent of crape jasmine
In this time of the year, lightening
Further the fragrant whispers of the breeze—
Where does she get off upstaging me?
Blooming Screw Pine—

Isn't it the welcome sign of changing season
With the first gust of thundershower that howls
through the night—

Wasn't it you who found sorrow
In the monotonous sound of rain drumming on the roof,
Intermittent flashes of lightning that illuminates the valley
Or was it the Parrot tree—

You or the insect chimes who first moaned,
lamenting—

Enter the valley any time you choose,
And stay there until the spring comes in

Ode To A Blackbird

The long-naked black bird veered,
hovered over the shallow pool of water
and landed with a loud splash,
creating ripples
that spreads in ever widening circles.
She floats there for a long time; ok slender neck
bobbing up and down, glancing sideways,
doing nothing. Occasionally she would dip in the water,
disappear completely, only to resurface a few frets away.
Then she lifted up to fly, wings flapping vehemently
causing a commotion in the otherwise placid
pool of water.
After she was gone, it seemed
the water would never stop shaking,
rising up and down in waves.
When it finally stopped moving, the waves diminished,
and the water becomes calm and flat again.

Agapanthus Africanus

In the winter warmth of our tiny conservatory
We're growing assorted herbs
And sowing hot chillis and sweet bell peppers.
But outside, way after Summer is over
And well past October and into November,
Long after her sisters have scattered their seeds
She heaves her proud head way up
Through her bed of tongue like leaves -
And there she now sits,
A proud queen adorned with a lilac coronet.
Buffeted by the now winter wind and rain
Of storm Bella -
An unwelcome yuletide visitor...
Agapanthus treats all adversity with disdain
And acts as a beacon of beauty in my backyard.
I don't know how long she will survive the coming months
Or whether she will live to see
Her new family of African Lillies this summer
When they push their tightly closed heads
Through their beds of moist earth once more.
But for now, in her small, sincere way
She's brought hope of renewal and survival
For the coming year ahead.

Aglaisurticae or Small Tortoiseshell Butterfly

She landed unseen on my garden dahlia
A multi-coloured beauty queen.
Bright orange against the vivid pink of the flower head
Spread wings with black spots, interspersed with yellow
And blue dots on the border.
When closed they are a mellow brown for camouflage
To avoid being eaten by a predator.
There she was, captured on camera
In all her glorious technicolour
Dipping her proboscis and sipping nectar
For all she's worth.
Gathering as much strength as she can muster
In order to propel her wings that will carry her
To the best cluster of stinging nettles in the area
On which she is destined to lay her precious clutch of tiny eggs.

Misumena Vatia (The Crab Spider)

She's a crab spider
Very apt if you live just a short walk from a beach
Just as I reached to water
A small yellow rose-bush
I spied her on a leaf
Her cowering and me towering over her.
She's white and very small
Only ten millimetres overall
With delicate markings on her back
Quite difficult to spot
And what she lacks in size
She makes up for her appetite
As with one bite
She can snare a honey bee for her tea.

The Boy Who Didn't Like Sand Between His Toes,

West Penwith, West where
The void and the epilogue
Open eyes at
Dusk, eclipsed, travelling like,
Like lava leaving lustful
Lisps on lips
Lost beyond lead red herring
Fleet lazy sails leaving,
Leaving me

The bristles that I
I sucked through troubled
Teeth carried weak,
And bold youth suddenly
Nowhere, where kings
Knew pharaoh's truths
Truths and fairytales

Honest prospect came
Came forward timely and
And awkwardly, I buckled
Shuffled and lied
Butter melted and
And yesterday got impregnated
Impregnated with
Tomorrow
By
Today.

I'll always be there

I'm thinking of you frequently
Praying for you too,
I pray that you are kept safe and well
Because in my books, you are swell,
The memories of us
In the back of my mind,
Will never fade away with time.
Even when I'm sound asleep,
My dreams and these memories seem to meet
Which makes me want to oversleep.
I'm thinking of you,
and I still care;
But I'm afraid that I might just tear.
We are both moving on,
And letting of the old story
But I'll admit,
It's scary.
We cannot change the past,
Yet, we can change how we deal with it.
I choose to find peace,
and keep the negativity to release.
I choose to heal,
Perhaps a new life
Will reveal.
Although we may be apart,
And our paths are going different directions,
I'm thinking of you,
and I still care;
So if you have any feelings you're wanting to share,
Just know,
I'll always be there.

Eavesdropping

Sitting on the bus,
conversations overheard,
range from family responsibilities in childcare,
and eyebrows,
or lack of,
the benefits of listening offers insights,
into lives unknown,
what's important and why simple honesty,
while quietly sitting on the bus.

The Dad Dilemma

Sitting in the garden and you in a hospital room.
Tenderness says I must visit you,
A reminder of better days,
Of the love buried in you.
A gentle gift to lift the haze.
A voice that brings passage from the vacuum.

Cowardice flinches at the visit that holds up the mirror
to the inevitable decay
of the end of days
and parting of ways.
The insurmountable losses further down the river.

It pains me to see you, a shadow of who you were,
A spectre biding your time.
It pains me not to see you, alone and confused, nowhere,
Waiting for the faces who ease time.

Tenderness and fear.
In softness, magnificent.
Malevolent with fear.
A fearful tenderness.

It is difficult to face you
when compassion is challenged by contempt.
Maybe I will face that demon
if I can bear the strain.
Maybe I am tired of demons
and the pain they ordain.
The cruelty served, so stonily indifferent.
Sitting with echoes of you.

Honourable Mention

To all the men I've loved and that one infatuation.
Whose charming presence caused a buzz of contentment.
For the reunions like illusions lightening disillusionment.
The ones who expressed their souls with such delightful flair.
The arms who held me so closely with healing loving care.
The babes whose eyes gleamed with visions of the man.
Who appeared in the turbulence to steady my hand.
The minds I ate with a spoon and asked for afters.
The humour, so attuned to insuppressible laughter.
The movements like the flourish of artistic mastery.
The discourse fanning the fancy of flattery.
The soothing support and easy encouragement.
The haven offered when the slaughtered spirit was spent.
Who saw the light when the dark kept me blind,
Revelling in the merry mischief of my mind.
Who built me up, sometimes, unintentionally.
The companionship that alters one so irrevocably.
Who loved the untamed ululations of the soul
And embraced the raw bareness with gentle console.
The crowned beats that blazed in the eyes.
The sweep of the feet that catches by surprise.
The yapping young and the fashioned of old.
The sterling silver and the grandiloquent gold.
Most highly honoured in the most thankful of hearts,
Who returned the esteem that so indelibly marked,
Who waved the souls colours in captivating celebration
beautifying life's revelations.

Magdalen

And when Compassion fails and we are left
abandoned in confusion and bereft
of all those heart-felt plaudits of pure love
what have we, at Life's End, to dwell above?
No more, think I, than any pig or goat
who, to the slaughter went by rote
and met an end unprecedented then
as any farmyard strutting cock or hen.
But words can maim and kill right here on earth
and leave us lives of none, or little, worth.
So shall I now guard well my Magdalen
and shield her from those jibes of mindless men.
Who knows what path ahead now lies for me?
Tomorrow is a wild uncharted sea.
A sea of word-pools and torment
but 'tis a choice from Heaven sent

Sometimes

Sometimes
I wonder why
my thoughts are all with
you being at my side.

So many times
you step into my dreams
you never seem to go away.

Please don't think
that I shall not honour what I pledge
that's not at all the way I am!

Just believe in me
and that day will soon be here
when our lives in harmony
will be the way
we'll have for evermore.

Solace

And now
the Final Day has come
one simple move into th'Eternal Sea
to float amongst the stars
and seek that longed-for path
where found will be all those
whom I have loved.

To be surrounded by
a Heaven of Love!
O Blessed Death

I do thee greet
with longed-for Desire
and now my loved ones
run to greet me –
O Sweet Death
O Solace!

Grief

I miss her voice
I miss her smell
I miss her lips
and what they could tell.

But most of all, I miss
her sense of humour,
that to others sounded daft,
but never failed to make me laugh.

I would like to buy this dress
for my dead wife,
if she was here right now
I'm sure she'd think it quite nice.

And perhaps a new pair of shoes
although I'm not sure of the style
that Angels use,
would a simple pair of sandals do?

She must need a warm coat quite soon
for when she stands in the garden
staring at me through the gloom,
surrounded by an ethereal glow
mouthing words that I should know.

I miss her voice, does she miss mine?
I miss her smell, can she still tell?
I miss her lips on mine, all of the time
I regret the breaking of the spell.

Whenever I see her standing there
I want to run my fingers through her hair.
With my nose pressed against the pane,
I stand as though frozen,
until her ghost at last
fades once more into my past.

The Road of Life

When I left home to join the road of life
I took no clothes, nor childhood bundle
but hung upon my belt a whetted knife
and left the road to go into the jungle.

To my left and right I hacked the jungle back
carving a path along which no one had spoken.
I never turned back, sweating in my jungle hat,
to look at the path I had so laboriously broken.

When arriving back, at the place I began
I slashed at the ground in my despair
realising that I was a man without a plan
and needed to get the hell out of there.

I would look up instead of looking down
setting my eyes on the mountains before me.
I climbed over the roughest of ground
giving my soul the chance to float free.

Then the Rucksack began breaking my back
and my feet felt blistered and broken.
I stopped for a rest, slipped off the pack
and waited for God's words to be spoken.

Hobbling down the mountain, in disgust,
I thought going on a quest was something to do
but not a thing, that you can really trust
and may in the end, do absolutely nothing for you.

The road of life can sometimes be a real sod,
so just keep plodding onwards, day after day
don't walk backwards on road you have trod
and laugh a lot with those you meet on the way.

Palms

The celebration of chaos & confusion,
daytant for the dark triad.
Unawakened possibilities &
perverted opportunities.
The volume is up &
the subtitles are clearer now.
Smother your heroes &
ignore your deities a new agenda &
a brighter day has been dictated from up above.
Shattered cheekbones,
black tongues, collapsed lungs &
slender threads of forgiveness are
dispensed by Sister Nigredo &
the Ministry of her presence.
The tormentor with no lips a permanent snarl
& a 1,000 yard stare.
Her voice once calm
now drips with falsehoods &
an intensive trust (the confidence).
Always check for the palms of your hands
when you're dreaming young man
because fear is the most subtle &
destructive of all human diseases.

Breathe/Repeat

The intrusiveness of those grey clouds
that muddle the psyche
& the black thoughts (ie: the Was Was)
that follow
& bypass the security
& fragility of our egos.
Into & towards the cold embrace
of self loathing
to be cradled by the familiar
arms of self doubt.

{Breathe}… the breath will appear.
{Exhale} to repeat >> again.

I harness the darkness presented to me
as if it was my chariot
while I navigate & make haste
through the country roads in the dead of night
watched over by the
Silver monocle
from the Moons paternal gaze.

The Beaufort Scale

Devised in 1805 by the Irish hydrographer Francis Beaufort (later Rear Admiral), a Royal Navy officer, while serving on HMS Woolwich.

The Beaufort Scale is an empirical measure for describing wind velocity based mainly on observed sea conditions.

Without regard for life or limb,
The weather, it comes storming in.
The waves do build, the wind does wail
As the weather climbs the Beaufort Scale.

From Force Zero to Fresh Breeze, Force Five
It's easy sailing and fairly calm
Stay alert but it's great fun to be alive
Certainly nothing to cause alarm.

But…

At Force Six, Strong Breeze, large waves with foam
The fishing fleet starts to think of home
At Seven, Near Gale, the foam does streak
Out-doors is no place for the weak!

At Eight, Gale, waves are eighteen feet,
And cars veer across the street!
At Strong Gale Nine, the slates do fly,
And chimneys shake against the sky.

At Ten, Whole Gale, whole trees do go,
And whole roofs too, "Look out below!"
Force Eleven, Violent Storm, thirty seven foot waves,
And has taken many to their graves!

But Force Twelve has another dread name,
And that dread name is Hurricane!
Ninety miles an hour winds, sixty foot seas,
Will do with you just what they please!

And wind and wave can go much higher,
If I told you now you'd think me liar!
But in the shriek and wave and wail,
You'll pray to God that you prevail!

And when it's over you won't believe
This friendly breeze knocked you to your knees.
You count your dead, lay them away
And brace to face another day.

But remember when fishers head away,
And sailors seek a sheltered bay,
When the weather is unfit for all,
The Life-boat is ready for your call!

Those brave, brave men will always sail
No matter what the Beaufort Scale.
They'll do their best for you and me,
And all in peril on the sea!

Dad

There is a crack in the sky
Where my Dad shines through
When I mention his name
I think of Mum too

They were a daily gift
And always will be
Hopefully smiling and waving
But definitely watching me
I wonder sometimes
When my turn will come
And I'll be up there
alongside the rain and the sun
With my mum and my dad
and so many who have passed
We will all be together
Reunited at last

Simplicity

I haven't written or even created anything for a while
seems a shame when it was my way to be busy, work and smile.
Depression meanders into your brain
and it languishes there 'til you crush it again
It eats you, it confuses you and it messes with your head
until the only safe place to be for me, was tucked up in bed.
I am writing this simply with no wisdom or class
just things that I think and feelings that will last.
I cannot seem to shed it or just explain things away
though I try to talk myself into doing one thing every day
I want to find myself again to not worry or fret
it has been 5 or 6 months – but there's no change in me yet.
The days can be low and quite hard to live in
and some can be level and I feel like I can win.
I really just want to be me, to be like before
to see people, travel and enjoy being outdoors.
Your prescribed medication should help you get back
to the person you were before starting to slack
It takes quite a time to recover and throw
the depression away and to let yourself glow.
People tell me 'take time, do not rush how you are'
So I am taking it easy, progressing slowly so far
hoping that the depression will leave me in time
and I can face each day again, full of hope and feeling fine

Flower Within

I couldn't really help it
And even if you'd told me not to
I would have done it anyway
Stealing from the garden
They never stayed around long enough
For me to paint in detail
So this is how I painted them
The flower
Yet I realised somehow I was painting me
In them their youth and beauty
Vitality before we age
Me and the flowers, we were the same
And I would have done it anyway,
I would have picked them even if you'd told me not to

Verdant Temple

Flowers opened in the moonlight
Had we walked here before?
In truth we only got to the gates of the orchard
It was protected by strong iron bars
I peered through to the place people do not walk in
I knew it would never leave me
Through the gates I saw the trees
The peace of wild things in the curved tulip wood
The still evening and the orange sun
Made everything dusky pink
A moment in time
I felt I'd be here again
I still think of it now

In God's House

There are the faithful few
who work unseen
and unobtrusively give of their best
Who spend their lives perfecting little things
which often pass unnoticed by the rest

There are the hands that dust the alter rails
that change the flowers and keep the linen fair
they sweep the aisles with cheerful reverence
and polish silver with murmured prayer

These are the quiet ones, who freely give
their time and thought and love with glad accord
who tread the byways of resolve,
and share the peace of God for their reward.

Black Sheeps

From a photo of two walkers
another soul connected with me million miles distant
he didn't have to say much
yet two words just soldered into me in an instant
"Black Sheep" key to my kindred soul.

The black sheep wondering under
under a canopy – that daren't share light,
appetite is one that none can be
as the darkness leaves the strongest to survive and wonder

The one that he was born in and under,
the tree in the forest so big and tall,
that nothing can grow or thrive,
yet moss and vines creep up the tree to catch a little light,
and never will be independently rooted of their own
because the forest's law so.

The black sheep found me on the edge of his shade,
in a random act of will
yet two words soldered into me
to throw him my hand and bring him to
Mayar Akash's light of the "Lovable Sky".

The light, will light up "you" in the forest,
the forest of you, where you will have your own canopy
and stand tall with your fruits or berries and bees
because of the emulation of Will's light
through the Loveable Sky.

What a reaction to an action, all this because the black sheeps
connected from a photo of two walkers.

Horse Whisper

And didn't she whisper?
She did. She didn't say much.
But what she imparted was more than enough room to hang yourselves
by yer foot from the tree whose each separate leaf is a history
of the nations of the world since before time began

She pawed the earth and raised her haunches
and pitied my sorry human ignorance
A half-assed two-legged who could never know the delights
of a four-hoofed canter, let alone a prairie gallop
the dust rising just before thunder and pouring rain,
with the lightning forking and the maverick rearing magic
beneath the first and last purple red blue green yellow rainbow's call
And the wild herd cantering, weaving across heaven's billowing
between dawn and sunset, the clouds like Ghost Riders In The Sky.

Quiet

for Jan Beaver Gallione

She had given everything for him
She had believed him
The mud drying on her skin
Night left
Dawn's bright day
Darkening her morn
She realized he had reneged
Not on her
Not even on the world
But upon himself
She could see
There in the X Ray
Of his heart
The frozen emotion
The frozen fear of...

Commentary:
"What happens next then?"
asks Aphrodite
"Well, it's a serial, innit?"
Says the Native American Contrary

Between them twin Ravens, Thought
And Memory got it sussed
Up above in their ever-open
Gilded cage the Ravens hang
Quiet

Queens Head!

When my grandfather
visited the English land,
my mum was just a teenager.
He took few queens head
with him to back home.
Young Elizabeth in copper and bronze.
Mum saves those in a trunk
for grandfathers memory.
We siblings grown up
with beautiful crowned Queen!

Half a century later
I came to English land.
Searching that young charming
and minted Elizabeth!
Holding the current coin of Queen
I find her jaded and weak!
But is still standing
and glittering like a crown
with devotion duty and responsibility.

The Moon

The moon's vibes flood through my wall,
There's no way to stop her at all,
She's in my blood and in my head,
Flooding me with dreams from toe to head.

Full moon today comes out to play,
Making me think in a different way.
Messages in my head, telling me the way ahead,
She speaks to my heart- that's my deepest part.

The messages are so strong,
Life changing and switch a beautiful song.
Glowing all around,
If we just let her shine,
The path we follow,
Will unwind.

I Haven't Got a Clue

What's the time?
I haven't got a clue,
Can I make a rhyme?
I haven't got a clue.

What's to do?
I haven't got a clue,
Where's my shoe?
I haven't got a clue.

Where are my glasses?
I haven't got a clue,
Where's my brain?
I haven't got a clue,
Am I insane?
I haven't got a clue.

Why am I writing am I writing this,
I haven't got a clue,
What am I supposed to do?
I haven't got a clue.

I don't know if your fed up yet?
I haven't got a clue,
When is it time for me to stop?
I haven't got a clue.

Should I get my coat and go?
I haven't got a clue,
That's the end,
I'll pass it over to you.

Reflections

When I look in the mirror,
Do you know what I see ?
A counterfeit image of duplicity.

I kick against structure,
Within it I thrive,
The parameters set,
To progress and survive.

I crave and seek kindreds,
Like minded collaborative,
But fear loss of control,
And claim back my narrative.

I challenge these boundaries,
But remove those restrictions?
I'm raw an exposed,
With all my conflictions.

A change of reflection,
Another person I see,
Are you an extension,
Or reinvention of me.

A different perspective,
Can I trust this is true?
Can I drop expectations,
And unmask with you.

Summer Solstice

Hope grows,
with a cadence,
of a ticking clock.

My tides full,
with anticipation,
Solstice my mountain peak.

Waxing and waning,
tipped light to dark,
Mazey to Montol.

My leaves begin to fade.

The Day

The Day has begun again,
What will happen today?
Will I achieve what I want?
Or shall I end the day with a grunt,
I step outside to do my usual chore,
Once I've done that I will then close the door,
And wander briefly into town,
Wearing my favourite summer gown,
Today is yet another day of the year,
Time to go back home now I fear.
I

Love retreats

Love retreats deeper into
our hollow shell,
A smouldering ember in
the darkness of our soul,

The flame gone,
the ember hides from the
pain, vowing never to
live again,

Smouldering and
smoking in this shallow
life, awaiting our break
up or down,

She hides there in our
heart, waiting, waiting,
waiting, for us to come
Home,

Painting by Numbers

If I was to attempt to paint this scene, I'd start
With the distant sky, that would gradually lose
Its rich cobalt,
Washed down
To its tidal sigh.

For those wispy flecks of cloud,
I'd try some gouache,
Flicked to show the tails trailing
And their racing manes,
That chase,
Then let them go.

For the sea;
I would have take some time to catch
Its blue mood vast,
In greys that cling under light half seen,
As stampedes, overhead
Pass.

The land next;
But what shades of green
Have been used to fuse in yellows and blues?
Tall grass,
Like the flowing hair
Of whose young face;
Head back, eyes closed,
Drinks in
This sun all day.
Breathes long on salt, and fern and hay.
While the cut fields yield to gold ambers,
Parallelograms edged by neat chamfers
Of short stone walled, adverse cambers
As patchworked,
Dog-eared, scrapbook pages
From
Where I sit up here.

The cattle; heads down are all facing north,

How strange and how clever
That they graze always
In unison,
As they amble silently,
Together.

To the cluster of buildings around Morvah church
That look to be leaning in,
To hear the soft Irish tones of St Bridget
...Kildare whispers in the wind.
The roof stones facing right, shine silvery white.
Drop a little sapphire,
Or cornflower, with the hint of a blush.
Not many buildings out here that require,
The tip of a brush,
There's just enough
Evidence of human involvement,
To make it relatable, sustainable and solvent.
But predating the otherwise mass colonisations
Those gross urbanisations,
Great swathes of occupations.
How could anything be amiss down there,
Comforted by the seas,
In the miniaturized distance,
And soothed by the gently shushing,
Scented breeze.

The foreground's textured pinks and yellows,
That require of my pencil's
Sharp scratches and etches,
Recording the raptured, unfolding credentials.
So much to capture;
A caterpillar clawing its way through the grass,
Do include him (or her)?
Its velvety, plump softness, rippling through its new body
That mellows,
In tiny, shiny hairs.
Is it brown or grey?
No,
More like carefully worked copper fading to divide
Into olivey blue,
With sharp flecks of creamed ivory down each side.

And then there's you;
My brush and pencil,
My keyboard and pen still fail me
After all this time, it's crazy.
And though I try, these rhyming words
...are mere words.
The echos and chiming, blurs
The reality;
As dynamic as you are caring
As you are considered
As you are daring.
No. Words and paints fall short
Though not through a lack of love
Or staring.

So much to narrate,
So much perfection to recreate.
Too much to acclaim in this single frame,
Yet this momentary scene
Will fall or stand
On a miracle of happy accidents.
And I'm afraid, too many
For this failing,
Mortal hand.

Sagres Sunset

The shimmering ball is lowered,
into sheets of Turkish blue,
that quietly softens the horizon,
this perspective and my view.

Ridges edged in deeper amber,
Persian orange drips off shelves,
 so that all that's in the farness,
gives what's left to Zavial.

Before the glow that pulls from Sagres,
turning turbines in a copse,
over hills that run to Aljezur,
deep teal is all but lost.

Now all the sea is breathing easy,
crickets chirp and swallows flee.
I've no idea how we got here.
What significance is me?

Another roll of this poor planet,
Moorish sunset's got me bad.
For if her fate were in safe hands,
there'd be no reason to feel sad.

The Beauty Between Beauty And Beauty

Beauty is you who lifts like the Wind,
Duty is mine to write the dust.
Green are your eyes that shine in my heart,
Unseen are the virtues that dwell within yours.
Blue are the skies that remind me of you,
True is the love that grows in my soul.
Mighty your beauty,
it chases the night,
Flighty is all that stands in your way.
Hands like the Heavens that hold until dawn,
the strands of my heart that lie within yours.
Eyes like the Night,
holding me Tight,
flies like the hours before the dusk.
Thinking of you in these moments of night,
sinking beneath the waves of your Beauty.

Benjamin Mathew John Haddy

When Infinity rains
it's calico drops upon the Golden Sun,
like the marble ashla passed before the chisel or
the breaking of the bread at Sundown
before the candle flame.

For the evening bell,
it now tolls
for he who has fallen
before his time
and left but a curtain of tears
for all who knew and loved him.

But if hands
that catch the tears that fall,
could also have
caught the man who fell,
who never knew
that Love and Hope,
is always at hand
for those like him,
who Lived
and Loved
and Hoped.

Ode To Alana

Here comes Xuaenruf Anala,
parking her powdered slippers by the Pussycat
and piercing her pencils by the ribbon,
her computer, it shines in the candle flame.

The antique robot,
he sips his glass of mercury
and dreams of pick pocketing Mona Lisa's credit cards
by the digital sunrise and hacking

Plato's Facebook account
before the pixelated dawn,
but otherwise banging southwardly
along the Iron Rail
in a world where the wind
rolls like waves
and the ships of war
with butterfly sails
are seen by Goldilocks Theodore,
but Goldy locks the door upon the beauty of it all,
for it overwhelms us
with its Golden Sun at Sundown,
it's fruit upon the bowl of bronze,
it's white capped evening waves,
her Eyes of Love
and the way the Summer evening wind
breathes with her and her smile.

Schindler's Gist

I never did get Schindler's Gist
as Schindler went shopping
with Shindler's List.
Schindler bought a watch,
it went on Schindler's Wrist.
Then Schindler went to the pub,
now Schindler's Pissed
and Schindler played some cards,
it was Schindler's Whist
and Schindler's Dissed
and Schindler saw Red
through Schindler's Mist.
"I'm gonna get a gun!"
Schindler Hissed
then Schindler took aim,
but Schindler Missed
and then Schindler had a fight
with Schindler's Fist.
Schindler met a girl
and Schindler's Kissed
and Schindler had a romance,
Schindler's Thrist
now Schindler's married
and Schindler's Blissed...
Turns out that she was a scaffolder
from Sloughs, Schindler's Twist!

Stormy Seas

As a wander in the sun and wind
round the coastal paths,
the weather changes
and blows a gale,
the sea so rough
the spray hits your face
and leaves that salty taste,
a wetness upon your face.

The roughness
somehow makes you calm,
wet to the bone,
cold with a shiver
as you venture home.

I took myself out
in that heavenly weather,
Nice to get home
legs like ice!
Face numb with the cold!

Lovely hot drink,
And the hottest of showers!
Warms the skin
and the hot drink warms within,
as the shivers subside!

Curl up in a ball in a blanket
to keep snug and warm.
Nice to be inside
out of the storm.

Life

Life is what you make it,
Should be full of fun,
Go find some joys,
Happiness in the sun.
Do what you love,
Go and enjoy,
There's a world of opportunity,
Take everyone.
The short time we are here,
A blink of an eye,
Only you have your choices,
Be careful and choose and be wise.
Have no regrets, see each day for what it is,
When our time is at an end,
Have you for-filled all your dreams,
Take the chances, join the ride,
knowing you had the very best life
and the best time,
then we can have that peace
knowing you enjoyed your time.

Time

Time is everything
you can have a
lot of time
or not much
so treat this
Day as the
last time
you have
left.

Waking up

I opened one eye
and check for the time
I reach for my glass
empty of course.

Put one foot gingerly to the floor
I pull myself up and grab open the door.

The sun is flooding through open blinds
I feel my heart lift
my spirits soar.

Come on, hurry,
get out of the door.

Through The Window

Snowflakes spun wildly
dancing and swirling

The moon, yellow,
full and round.

Nearby, a dog howled,
baying to the moon.

The trees,
a dark silhouette
against the silent white blanket of snow.

Beauty, all around.

Silently,
through the window.

Nature

I wonder lonely
as a cloud
in the open,
where the weather was fair
in the open air.

I sat in the open air
having a picnic in the field,
over there,
where it takes you there.

Conversations from Imagination

To love and to be loved is everything.
You have so many good qualities.
You are caring, loving, sharing, giving,
doing something special,
doing something different,
making your loved one
feel that they are special and unique,
they are the best!
Anyone would pray,
would do anything to have you in their life.
Anyone would consider themselves fortunate to
have you in their life.

However, I am not that person.
I don't like to be cared, loved, getting gifts,
I don't like to get any special treatments
or even feeling...
I get frustrated, I get tired and bored...
I am frightened of your presence,
I am frightened of your voice;
I am fearful that you could come out from my imagination,
you could be front of me at any moment.
If I see you, I am not only nervous but also panicky -
I don't want to lose you ever.
Please don't leave me alone.
I can't live without you.

The Disillusioned Young Mum

No I don't want to eat any carrots
no I don't want to see in the dark
no I don't want to grow up big and strong
and I'll never get caught by the snark.

No I don't think it's way past my bedtime
I don't think that boogies exist
there's nothing upstairs now in the dark
that in the light I have missed.

No I don't want my hair combed and face washed
I don't think anyone will care
that a dried up trail leads from my nostrils
and into the ends of my hair.

Affairs of the heart

My secret boatman comes to me
offering love and company
my most delicious secret he
with feelings to set my spirit free
from home and work and family
my delicious secret boatman he.

The Winds of Change

The winds of change can be insane
As Politicians gnaw on the bones of lies and putrid piles of policies.
Stagnant turgid wheels of civil servants grinding towards their self inflated
pensions.

The tension of the poor twists and pulls the hate and frustration of a nation on its
knees.
Please, Please vote for me MPs implore from their bus of hope.
All aboard, they smile and wave.
Then drop you off at your early grave.

Yet still you strive to keep a semblance of normality, stunned by the new
immorality.
The Artificial Intelligence stopped making sense when drones and phones and
loans and debt, fillers and killers, fake solutions to pollutions, that smother every
mother, every brother in a smog.
That's spreading like a virus descending to MINUS because of MIDAS.
The yoke of the dollar weighing round your collar. Blinkered with phones and
screens eyes down hypnotised my memes and fake schemes. Enticing teens with
fake lashes and nails and boobs and lips.

Why trust in the youth to fight for the truth? When the beauty of their humanity
has been marred by profanity, deception at inception.
Rare seeds of hope grow slow in the land of the comfort zone.
Yet preparation of the nation resistant to change, continues undaunted.
No space for reflection, just decorations like United Nations,
Space Stations and Value creations.
Rights For All! The big and the small! The bold and the old!
Desire to succeed, need for speed!

Recharge your car while you are at the bar,
drinking a toast to the one with the most.
Let no man put asunder our fight for the right to plunder!

Your Smile

The Sunshine of your smile started to melt
the icicles of sorrow weighing heavy in my heart.

The heat of your kisses,
like butterflies brushing my skin.

Shivers of delight ran through my body
and the fires of desire rose dancing.

My spirit soared
and an ancient thudding Rhythm of love began.

The vibrations of your soul
struck a chord deep in my heart.

Like a phoenix rising from the ashes of a long sleep,
a blue flame shot across the stars
cascading silver showers of joy.

Heritage-less

As my mother sings
her Welsh songs
in our Cornish town

my eyes trade with sky
(while the stewardess checks my ticket)
asking for something akin to a death place

but sky crosses her clouded legs
and offers nothing
but my own blank flag.

Phyllis calls from her room

Phyllis calls from her room,
shouts:
'HELP ME! HELP ME!
HE'S HERE AGAIN
AND HE WANTS ME TO SING TO HIM!'

I turn off her bell
ask, 'who's there, Phyllis?'
She shouts:
'THE ONE WHO DIED!
HE'S HERE NOW
AND HE WANTS ME TO SING!'

'Will you?' I ask
and she looks at me with her 90-year-old eyes
sighs out 90 years of songs
and sings.

Her voice breaks at every word
like she's too tired to sing the next verse.

When she's finished
she's more than alive
and I can see how young she is
behind those eyes.

She turns to me and shouts, 'YOUR TURN,
SING TO ME MY LITTLE GIRL,
MY CHILD, MY SWEETHEART, MY LOVELY DARLING,
SING TO ME MY LITTLE STARLING!'

I sing to her
and I stroke her hair -
her barely-there hair
soft as air.

Probably

Because Coventry is really a synonym for depression.
So when he tells me he is in Cov
I do not ask how he is.

+ I go back there, metaphorically like, I'm not stupid,
+ I see it
in all its grey walls + skies + pavements +
people walking around in grey clothes + skin + faces.

The dog tug-tug-tugs
to sniff the side of a streetlamp I imagine has been pissed on
+ there he is
standing
with a tattoo on his arm of Mary, Mother of God
+ I know it's weird but I couldn't help asking,
Do you believe in God?
+ he said probably
+ stroked the dog's black, black head.
Tells me he sees me
take this walk every day
alone
+ am I lonely?

I say sometimes
+ he walks around Lady Herbert's Gardens with us.

When we sit down he cups the dog's head
tells me
that the black dog has got him. Sometimes
he sleeps for days on end + when he wakes up + goes for a piss,
it is almost black.
I squint at him because the sun is beating it fists on his blonde, blonde head
+ when I try to see his eyes
they are just reflections.

He asks me for a rizla but I don't smoke.
If you ever want to talk, he tells me, I'm usually here
+ points to the Transport Museum
its grey walls swamping the sun.

Mellow

When I was small
I sat beneath the willow tree
in the back garden.
It cast a shadow on the pond
and until I was embarrassingly old,
I truly believed there was a crocodile
in there, waiting for me.

I used to tap the soles of my jelly shoes
on the surface
tap
to tempt him
tap
secure in my belief
tap
that no matter what happened,
my mother was bigger and stronger
than anything that could have snapped out of that pond
tap.

And of course,
when make-believe made its way
into the light of day,
my mother would say:
keep believing in that crocodile,
take it with you as you grow.
You might need something unreal
to face this world of woe.

Index

A Different World - By Penny Collins   10
A Dream Of Night House - By Leema Begum   16
A Friendship Bursts - By Leema Begum   45
Affairs Of The Heart - By Kim Bastian   100
Agapanthus Africanus - By Pam Turner   52
Aglaisurticae Or Small Tortoiseshell Butterfly - By Pam Turner   53
Aroma of Garlic - By Bea Thompson   24
Beauty - By Anthony Craig Oats   32
Benjamin Mathew John Haddy - By Leo Rudman   89
Bits - By Adrian Dudley Fost   13
Black Sheeps - By Mayar Akash   74
Breathe/Repeat - By T. M. Warren   66
Broken Heart (A Prayer) - By Jonathan Hayter   44
Conversations From Imagination - By Ayesha Choudhury   98
Dad - By Libby Pentreath   69
Eavesdropping - By Sonja Fairfield   57
Flower Within - By Francesca Owen   71
Found Myself - By Ayesha Choudhury   33
Grief - By Robert Cardwell Spencer   63
He Rebel - By Mukut Borpujari   19
Hear Me - By Joanna Edwards   39
Heritage-Less - By Nicole Paton   103
Honourable Mention - By Nayma Chumchun   59
Horse Whisper - By Adrian Dudley Frost   75
I Haven't Got A Clue - By Alan S. Whitfield   79
I'll Always Be There - By Zainab Khan   56
In God's House - By Valerie Kaute   73
Jump - By Alan S. Whitfield   21
Life - By Christine Jilbert   93
Like The Child You Are - By Angie Butler   31
Love Retreats - By Alan S Whitfield   83
Magdalen - By John Cynddylan   60
Mellow - By Neil Graham Oats   29
Mellow - By Nicole Paton   106
Mental Hospital - By Keith Woodhouse   11
Misumena Vatia (The Crab Spider) - By Pam Turner   54
Mother's Funeral - By Mary Fletcher   49
Nature - By Anthony Craig Oats   97
Night Poem - By Joanne Edwards   38

No More - By Daniel Muunn   28
No Time To Say Goodbye - By Valerie Kaute   26
Ode To A Blackbird - By Mukut Borpujari   51
Ode To Alana - By Leo Rudman   90
Pain - By Joanna Edwards   12
Painting - By Numbers By Rob Kersley   84
Palms - By T.M.Warren   65
Phyllis Calls From Her Room - By Nicole Paton   104
Probably - By Nicole Paton   105
Profile - By Keith Woodhouse   34
Purpose - By Christine Jilbert   27
Queens Head! - By Opu   77
Quiet - By Adrian Dudley Frost   76
Reflections - By Rosie Beale   80
Sadly Love Is Never Enough - By Angie Butler   35
Sagres Sunset - By Rob Kersley   87
Schindler's Gist - By Leo Rudman   91
Shaman Dalang - By Jonathan Hayter   14
Simplicity - By Libby Pentreath '23   70
Solace - By John Cynddylan   62
Solstice Haiku - By Rosie Beale   22
Sometimes - By John Cynddylan   61
Spring - By Mukut Borpujari   50
Stormy Seas - By Christine Jilbert   92
Summer Solstice - By Carol Rea   81
The Beaufort Scale - By Res Burman   67
The Beauty Between Beauty And Beauty - By Leo Rudman   88
The Black Lake (From A Dream) - By Jonathan Hayter   43
The Boy Who Didn't Like Sand Between His Toes - By Vivian Pedley   55
The Dad Dilemma - By Nayma Chumchun   58
The Day - By Suzette Reed   82
The Disillusioned Young Mum - By Kim Bastian   99
The Drowning Man - By Carol Rea   23
The Dust Storms Of The Soul - By Jonathan Hayter   41
The Legend Of Port Quin - By Res Burman   42
The Moon - By Alan S. Whitfield   78
The Point - By Julie Flowerdew   30
The Road Of Life - By Robert Cardwell Spencer   64
The Sun Scores Its Silver Blade - By Angie Butler   36
The Trapeze Artist - By Pam Turner   20
The Winds Of Change - By Ruth Husbands   101
They Should Have Done It Yesterday - By Angie Butler   37

Through The Window - By Julie Flowerdew 96
Tiger - By Leema Begum 46
Time - By Daniel Munn 94
Train Travel - By Mary Fletcher 48
Tribute - By Lowenna Helen Kaute 25
Unconditional Love From 1943 - By Chloe Hall 17
Verdant Temple - By Francesca Owen 72
Vision - By Keith Woodhouse 15
Waking Up - By Julie Flowerdew 95
Wolf's My Feet - By Joanna Edwards 40
Your Smile - By Ruth Husbands 102
Yum, Yum, Yum! - By Leema Begum 47